Gus
the Pup

By Marcie Aboff
Illustrated by Nuri Vergara

Scott Foresman
is an imprint of

Glenview, Illinois • Boston, Massachusetts • Chandler, Arizona •
Upper Saddle River, New Jersey

Photographs

Every effort has been made to secure permission and provide appropriate credit for photographic material. The publisher deeply regrets any omission and pledges to correct errors called to its attention in subsequent editions.

Unless otherwise acknowledged, all photographs are the property of Pearson Education, Inc.

8 Ariel Skelley/Getty Images.

ISBN 13: 978-0-328-50753-5
ISBN 10:   0-328-50753-9

9 10 V010 15 14 13

Gus is our new pup.

He rides in our car.

He comes to our house.

Gus is our new pup.

He is a good pet.

He is very cute!

Gus is our new pup.
He needs dishes of food
and water.

Gus is our pup.

He goes to a school for dogs.

He learns not to run away.

Gus is our new pup.
He likes to play with his
friends.

Puppies

When puppies are first born, they drink their mother's milk. When they are about five weeks old, they're ready to eat puppy food, as long as it's soft and easy to chew. Healthy puppies grow fast. They need food, water, exercise, regular naptimes, and lots and lots of love!